T0381297

SILICON VALLEY AND TRAVEL TIPS

C.MCKENZIE- KIELY

AuthorHouse™
1663 Liberty Drive
Bloomington, IN 47403
www.authorhouse.com
Phone: 1 (800) 839-8640

Published by AuthorHouse 10/27/2018

ISBN: 978-1-5462-6557-3 (sc)
ISBN: 978-1-5462-6556-6 (e)

Library of Congress Control Number: 2018912790

Print information available on the last page.

FOREWORD

My name is Chris McKenzie Kiely. This material is my book. I am very fortunate to have spent most of my working career in Silicon Valley. I have written about my work experience as well as my experience in Silicon Valley and elsewhere. I have traveled extensively and included that information with this material. I hope you will be enlightened.

DEDICATION

· ·

This book is dedicated to Michael Joseph Christopher Kiely without whom I never would have released it.

Author at Intel Museum

A favorite expression at Intel Corporation, Santa Clara, Silicon Valley, was "If it is not broken, break it." I remember a lot of people having this quote on their lips. In other words, if something is working right, you should try to improve on it. Most Silicon Valley employees, "think outside the box." Another thing you never heard was "that's not my job." When Silicon Valley employees find something not working, they should find someone to fix it, or fix it themselves. What is really nice about being an employee in Silicon Valley is you are usually on the edge of something big. I found employees came in early, worked through lunch and worked late. They really liked their jobs. Everyone had a cubical, even the president of Intel. You were made to feel like you could talk to anyone, of any authority, about anything. Also, you only needed one wardrobe in Silicon Valley. Most people dressed casually and I even saw a high-ranking executive in shorts one day. The weather is usually nice. Which reminds me; if you have a staff meeting, or meeting of any sort, you might have it outside. President Andy Groves of Intel would sometimes make his rounds talking to people to see what was going on at all levels. I'm sure Andy had a private place to meet for secret meetings but everything was kept very transparent. Many managers in Silicon Valley hire people that have been working only three to five years at another company. Their thinking is that a person becomes bored in their job, wants a change, doesn't have a way up and isn't learning anything new after three to five years at another company. So, you might have a person in their twenties who has already worked at two or three companies in Silicon Valley.

I had friends who kept calling me from Westinghouse, Sunnyvale, Silicon Valley, who said I would love to work there. After Westinghouse promised to pay for my master's degree as soon as I started, I agreed to work there. Northrup Grumman bought

Westinghouse, so I was sitting in the same seat for two companies. I was recruiting engineers to work on projects. Can you believe that there is a train that rides around all over the United States, that looks like a normal train, but is a defense unit that Westinghouse made. If something threatening enters our airspace, that train can shoot it down. Congresswoman Nancy Pelosi visited our site to find out how much funding we needed to complete projects we were working on. After a successful visit, our CEO told us we better vote if we wanted to hold onto our jobs. Most people in Silicon Valley go by their first names. Some people like to have "Doctor" said in front of their name.

Lone Pine

The Lone Pine appears to grow through rock and it's on 17-Mile Drive, which is filled with mansions, seals on rocks and Pebble Beach Golf Course, which is where Bing Crosby played and passed away.

Dr. Hackbert, Dean of National University in San Jose, Silicon Valley, contacted me and asked me to teach human resources at his university. He wanted me to be an adjunct professor and I said yes. San Jose State, Santa Clara University and Stanford University all probably required PhDs to be professors, so I was happy to be an adjunct professor for National University. I was teaching human resources and business courses to people trying to get their masters degrees. One engineer approached me and said he had to travel a lot on his job, so he would come to the tests, and that's all. I told him he would fail the class because participation was very important and he found a way to come to all the classes. A different time I was teaching effective presentation and a female student told me she couldn't speak in front of the class. I told her it was necessary for her to get a grade. We decided we would let her hold onto the podium when she spoke. As soon as she opened her mouth to speak, she fainted. We called an ambulance and she was oaky. Maybe I'm too soft, but I let her present to me alone and do some extra assignments and I let her pass the class.

If you live in Silicon Valley, you better get used to earthquakes. Silicon Valley has had several earthquakes. Me and a girlfriend were laying on our stomachs on the beach in our bathing suits between Santa Cruz boardwalk and the ocean when an earthquake occurred. Although it wasn't one of the bigger earthquakes it was a weird feeling having all the grains of sand move in all different directions. When there are earthquakes, radio stations ask you to call in and tell them what you were doing when the quake occurred. Also, many people look in big windows of stores like grocery stores to see what kind of damage happened inside. I remember our biggest quake while I was in Silicon Valley was in October 1989 during the World Series between the Giants and the A's. I was at working out at the company gym when it occurred. All of us people were down on the floor and we saw lights swaying back and forth. I looked towards the door and saw a guy washed out of our swimming pool onto the surrounding cement. I crawled out because no one could stand and checked on an employee who had just returned from a disability. Everything is competitive in Silicon Valley. What I mean is most businesses have a gym, and/or pool and a cafeteria to remain competitive with other employers. I got in my car to head home, and in case you didn't know, all cars feel like they have a flat tire when there is an earthquake. Earthquakes usually have many aftershocks, and this one was no different. Many cars were stopped in the road, so I stopped and parked mine and walked past the Winchester Mystery House and a lot of cars were there. The Winchester Mystery House is supposed to be haunted and the owner talked to a psychic after her husband died and was told to keep building on the house and she would keep living as long as she was building. Sarah Winchester was very wealthy and continued to be after her husband died because of the sale of Winchester rifles. She felt guilty because of all the souls who died because of Winchester rifles and continued to build until she died. She is long gone so the house is a museum that is open for tours. October is a popular month for touring there because of Halloween.

Santa Cruz Boardwalk

Meanwhile, back at work, I was sharing quality values with all the VPs on 9/11 when someone came into the conference room and said turn on the TV. We watched the TV as the second plane hit the second tower live. Everyone has a different hero that day. My hero is Norman Mineta. He stopped all the planes from flying that day until they checked them out. My understanding from someone who should know is this person saved a lot of lives because they found several bombs that were sneaked on to other planes that were prevented from taking off. I had a doctor who reported to me and he asked if he could go for a couple of weeks to pull bodies out of the towers. He used to be a green beret and it was one of his friends that told me about the bombs. I don't think I should release his name. I don't think he would appreciate it. Going back to the earthquake, let me say that I found out a lot about the earthquake after I passed the Winchester Mystery House. The mall next door had a café/bar with candles lit and a battery-operated TV, so I went in. Today a mall exists across from the Mystery House and it's called Santana Row. There are all kinds of shops and eating places there, and lots of people go there. I found out this was not like our regular earthquakes. It was televised, that even though the epicenter was under Los Gatos, most of the damage was done to people in cars on roads and bridges near San Francisco. People were dying. Inside the café were different people telling their stories of when the earth quaked. A guy told us he was opening a lingerie store when the quake hit and women ran out of the dressing room no matter how they were dressed or undressed. Another couple from L.A. was on a tour in the Mystery House and thought the quake was part of the tour. When I got home I found all the lamp shades had shimmied down, some windows broke that were going the direction of the quake, all the cabinets in the kitchen were open and the dishware had fallen out. Most houses in Silicon Valley don't have basements. So, when one hits, stand in a doorway or if you have an empty wine cellar, go down there. Never ever put anything above your bed. And it's a good idea to put latches on all of your cupboards. We walked around Los Gatos the next day to see all the damage and I kept my eyes peeled for Steve Wozniak, one of the founders of Apple. He lives in Los Gatos and has a license plate that reads "GO WOZ." I believe he has a Tesla now. He's real nice. If you wave, he will wave back. In Silicon Valley housing is very expensive. The rumor has it that you could buy a house there that costs twice as much as anywhere else in the United States. Houses by the beach are especially expensive. The more trees in the yard and the more private, the more expensive. A lot of people in Silicon Valley offer over asking price when buying a house to make sure they get it. Some people just buy a dilapidated house on nice property and mow it down to build what they want. Back at work the headhunters kept calling me with other opportunities in Silicon Valley. I kept saying no, until they mentioned Apple, then I said yes. I interviewed at Apple and got an offer. I copied the offer letter and laid it on my Boss's desk when he wasn't there. He came running to me and asked if I was leaving. I answered, you tell me if I'm leaving, because the offer was for a similar position, for a lot more money. My boss negotiated with me and I decided to stay. Apple called me and wanted to know when I was starting and I told them my answer to their offer was no, I was staying. The guy on the other end of the phone hollered "no one says no to Apple." Two other calls came from Apple. But I decided to stay where I was. This might be a good place to say what you can negotiate for when going to a new employer in Silicon Valley. You can always ask for more vacation, a bonus, earlier reviews, to a membership somewhere. There is not a limit in Silicon Valley, you can ask for anything. A common way to get new applicants besides advertising is to use Westech Services. Westech is where many companies go to showboat their openings and to meet possible applicants. I saw resumes from laborer's to engineers to the NASA employees who looked for other forms of life. A girlfriend who's a teacher wanted to go to Westech's last night party with me. I couldn't go and she was standing at the door looking for me. Rod Lake, who was a partner at Westech saw my friend and asked her if he could escort her to the right table. He asked her who she was and she gave my name and he just laughed and talked to her all night. He went along with her saying she was me until she admitted the truth at the end of the night. They both thought it was so funny.

Hearst Castle Pool

On the whole, people from Silicon Valley are very open-minded and non-judgmental. This reminds me of an employee of ours who was always coming to me for Human Resource issues. This time was different. He was wearing a dress and makeup and his hair was grown long. He told me the doctor was making him act like a woman for a year before he would do the operation to make him one. His issue was the bathroom. He didn't know if he should use the women's or men's bathroom, so we created a single bathroom for him and anyone could use it when he wasn't in it. He planned to stay with his wife and child because he still loved them and they loved him.

Silicon Valley people are very generous with their time and money. There are lots of things they do in their free time. I spent my time working with blind children, Meals on Wheels, and my favorite, crisis intervention counseling. The Red Cross taught us how to take calls from a variety of people. The call could be from latchkey kids, old people who just wanted to talk, people with illnesses people or lots of other including suicidal people. When one suicidal person called me, he said he had so much liquor and pills in his system he would be dead soon, but he wanted to talk to somebody when he died. After I was unsuccessful in getting his name and address, I turned the phone next to me upside down and called a dispatcher. He was slurring his words and I told the dispatcher to urgently trace the call and what was going on. He fell off of his chair and hit the floor and couldn't talk so I told him to punch the chair twice when he meant yes for questions I was going to ask him. I was asking him questions to keep him awake when I heard pounding at his door and the police breaking down his door and they hung up the phone. The dispatcher called me back and said the guy was unresponsive but had vital signs that might save him if he got to the hospital on time. I hope he is alive today.

It might seem odd to people outside of Silicon Valley, but Silicon Valley people have many ways that they spend their time. They may go to life coaches, masseuses, acupuncturists, manicurists, psychics, and other things. A Silicon Valley person might try anything once to see if it should be continued.

Headhunters were still calling me and when they finally talked about a place that would send me around the world resolving HR issues, I was interested. I interviewed at Harris, closer to San Francisco, I liked what I heard, so that was my next employer. I went to England to interview engineers. When I sat down with the man to interview him, his wife pulled up a chair as well. I was confused until they told me the spouses usually interviewed with their spouses to ask questions about benefits or whatever. What was awkward for me is I always asked candidates accomplishments as well as failures and how they could have been rectified. I got used to it.

***From here on out I intend to give you travel tips. I will pick the cities and countries where I had the best experiences and relay them to you. It's impossible to tell you about the cities and countries I've been to, so I'll try to pick the best.

England is so fun to experience and London is the best place of all. I'd suggest contacting London Walks to see the best of it. You'll get to see the Tower of London, Westminster Abbey, St. Paul's Cathedral and even where Jack the Ripper committed his crimes. You can visit one of the world's great wonders, which is Stonehenge and go to Harrods for all your shopping. Although London has become one of the worlds great food destinations, have the fish & chips for a taste of authentic food.

Picadilly Circus

Stonehenge

In Rome the tour guides will tell you not to take pictures of the Sistine Chapel. It could dull the art, which is beautiful. The Pope has a public audience every Wednesday where many languages are spoken. About six thousand people are in St. Peter's Square for the audience and we saw Pope Francis. He told everyone to hold up anything they wanted to have blessed. I saw Pope John Paul II in California and I brought my mother out from the East Coast to enjoy it with me. There are lots of shops to buy things and lots of museums and galleries to visit. There are two other places you must visit while in Rome. They are called the Spanish Steps and the Trevi Fountain. It was raining when I was there and they were still beautiful sights. The subway that brings you to the Coliseum has a nice restaurant which we tried and was tasty. We found that any pasta or pizza in Italy was good. In Rome there is a cat shelter called the Torre Argentina cat sanctuary. It's located in a ruin, right in the center of Rome. About 50 cats are there at any one time. You can visit them but don't feed them because they might follow you and get hit by a car.

Rome Cat Sanctuary

Spanish Steps

Pope arriving at the stage

In Paris there are architectural wonders. The Champs Elysees must be seen and many places to shop and eat are there. In Paris, desert is good no matter where you get it. Paris has a lot of expensive food, but that's not necessarily the best food. You can get good food anywhere in Paris. You must see the Louvre with its gorgeous art and see the Mona Lisa which is roped off so people don't get too close. We went to the top of the Eiffel Tour when it was daylight and when we came down all the lights were on because it's lit at night. Notre Dame is also very popular and you should see it while there. The are catacombs below the streets of Paris and we saw many thousands of skeletons while we toured there. The catacombs are there because they moved them from cemeteries to make room and stewards sat there to make sure tourists didn't make off with the bones.

Louvre

Mona Lisa

Eiffel Tower

I went to Germany because we had an excellent sales engineer, who was engaged to a woman who was afraid to move to Germany. She wanted to know she would be treated okay while married to him there because she was Jewish. I did a lot of digging and rumor has it the German people go out of there way to be extra nice to Jewish people because of their past. She married him, moved there and everything was hunky dory. It's best to go to Germany in September-October, that's when everyone is celebrating Oktoberfest and you might see a lot of people wearing Lederhosen and Dirndl dresses. Be sure to try the sausage, kraut and mashed potatoes in Germany. Pretzels in bars and beer gardens are huge, soft and covered with salt. I asked a waitress for ice for my drink and she told me never to order ice in Europe. Found out that ice is usually for storing dirty things and drinks are usually room temperature. I noticed most windows on homes had beautiful flower boxes beneath them. I wish everyone could try the autobahn. Riding on the autobahn is like riding in an amusement park ride. The taxi I was in regularly went over 100 miles per hour and we were still being passed by many cars.

In Brussels Belgium, I had a wonderful meal. Mussels and fries are a very popular dish. Belgium has some of the best beer in the world, some of it brewed it Trappist monks. The Belgians eat late with lots of wine. When I was getting ready to get my rental car, I found out it was locked up with many others. All cars are locked up around 7 or 8, to keep people from driving drunk. I had to get another hotel even though I didn't drink anything. The reason I was meeting an engineer for dinner, was because all summer was considered vacation in most of Europe, and I had to work out a solution between the engineers who got three weeks vacation or more in America. Working with bonuses, I resolved the issue.

Switzerland has beautiful scenery. Fondue is popular here and better than you get in the States. You must go to Lake Zurich and you must hear Zurich's symphony.

Amsterdam is a great place to visit. Try the pickled herring if you dare. It's good. What makes it really different is marijuana is legal in the coffee shops and people are allowed to go to the Red-Light district where prostitution is legal. You must visit the Ann Frank, Van Gogh and Rijks Museums.

The last place in Europe I'm going to give travel tips on is Spain. Although all countries in Europe are worth visiting I can only tell you about the ones I know. I was on a personal vacation in Miami and staying at the Fontainebleau Hotel which was made famous by Jerry Lewis in The Bellboy. My company called me on vacation and asked if I would go straight to Spain to get an engineer that they didn't want the competition to get first. I said yes and took a plane from Miami to Madrid. I went to lunch with several men and our candidate and I raised my coffee cup while they raised their wine glasses and said Salut! They all laughed and repeated Salut! Lunch is the biggest meal of the day for Europeans and it could be two to three hours long. I couldn't drink wine that day because I was recruiting and I had a big afternoon. The restaurants are decorative and the paella is what's best to eat. I call it my Spanish cioppino. A que is what they call a line of people in Spain. I went into a bank and walked straight up to an open window. I was an ugly American and the que started grumbling. They told me each person goes in the que when the come in. I also found out that most people put their tip as part its already on the receipt on the in the amount owed. A couple times I left more than the receipt said and was treated very amicably. You could go to a bull fight but I chose not to because I found out they weaken the bull they fight to ensure the matador is winning.

Now we're going to South America. I had a devise that you could talk into and on a screen it said what you said, in the local language. I took it everywhere with me. I would go to the book stores and get language arithmetic to understand the language in each country. Argentina had beautiful scenery and great places to eat, but what's worth writing about is Uruguay, Brazil and Colombia. I went to a movie in Brazil, where the language is Portuguese and subtitles were available. I ordered popcorn with lots of topping and was surprised to get popcorn with shredded cheese on top, so that's how Brazil eats its' popcorn.

In Bogota, Colombia my company told me to be aware because non-taxies disguised as real taxis were ripping off tourists. When I arrived, it was late and a man picked up my luggage and put in his car. I followed him and got in the back seat and he stopped the car in a very dark, isolated place and asked me what I planned on paying him. I said whatever your meter says and I noticed he didn't have a meter. I gave him more that I knew the trip was worth and he took me to my hotel. Everything else went well during that trip, but I swear I could hear shots fired every so often. When I came home from Bogota, the stopover was Miami and I noticed my luggage had been rifled through and there was a whole or two in it. I started to the baggage claim man and noticed my talcum powder was open and thrown about. They wouldn't let me near my luggage and brought out dogs. When everything was cleared, they told me that somebody could tell I had talcum powder in my luggage and that was often used to carry cocaine. I told the airline and the luggage attendant backed me up and I received all new luggage. I was glad to get home.

Next, I went to Mexico cut loose an employee. The law in Mexico is that you pay a fired employee for many months, so I hoped he'd be okay getting another job. I had an interpreter with me so there was no mix-up in the words. I also climbed steps of pyramids put there by the Aztecs years ago. The food in Mexico is similar to Mexican food in the States, but it's original there and I think it's better: burritos, enchiladas, etc.

I spent a lot of time in Asia. Some places I spent just a few days and some places I spent longer. When I was on a tour bus in Hong Kong, the tour guide told the whole bus that I was asking whether they still ate cats and dogs. She said people her grandfathers age still do, but younger people don't. Again, I felt like the ugly American. It is true that Hong Kong really makes counterfeits like authentic. The watches and purses are especially done well.

When I was in Japan, I bought some gold and the gold was a few carats more than I'd ever had before. The sales man said America isn't allowed to have carats that high, so I was happy to get it. You'll notice aquariums are popular. They are considered good luck.

Singapore is so neat and clean. Spitting gum on the sidewalk or writing graffiti is against the law. It's like that country has OCD, but it's beautiful and very, very clean.

I was told in the Philippines there are more Americans than any other nationality. I thought that was good. I found out that was because of all the American graves.

Kuala Lumpur, hereafter called "KL", is very conservative. They don't allow you to bring in any covers of magazines or ads, that depict a couple together or a woman scantily dressed. WE had a factory in KL and the manager walked me around. A man and two women were arguing. The manager told me that was a man and his two wives and that happens often. I saw a lot of monks and it's a very crowded country. The parking is at such a premium that I was forced to take a rickshaw a couple of times. I brought a candidate to one of our customers to interview and he stopped his car, pushed a car up and a car down so we could park. He said it's the law to leave your car in neutral so people could do that. I was warned to bow if the King came by. It was illegal not to. They didn't care where you were from, you went to jail. I was waiting for a written offer to be faxed to me but I couldn't tell the candidate until it arrived. I winked at the candidate and his fiancé to let them know it would be good news. They told me that winking there meant that I was a prostitute and ready for business. He was happy with the offer and they said yes. He also told me that crossing your legs towards a person was an insult. These are kinds of things you don't find out from a tour book.

The durian fruit is something you should try while in Asia, but it is banned in a lot of places. Some people say it's the best tasting fruit in the world, but has a negative odor when you cut into it.

I usually go on these trips alone, which takes a lot out of me, but sometimes two or three others may join me on the trips, but rarely. It was time to go home.

I thought I was done working and I was going to retire early, but I received an offer I couldn't turn down. I was asked to do a contract assignment for the Rand Institute in Santa Monica, and they are special in the world of employment. I was also asked to be an adjunct professor again in southern California at National University on Tuesday and Thursday evenings, and Saturday mornings.

I met a doctor that said he spent his summers in India helping Mother Theresa with people for free. He told me the last time he saw her, he spanked her lightly and told her to keep moving and she shook her finger at him and said "bad boy." I think he is a good person for helping for free over many summers, but I don't know he should have teased her like he did.

I rented an apartment in Beverley Hills, walking distance from Rodeo Drive, which is a great place to shop and those of you who have seen Pretty Woman know what I'm talking about. I was sorting resumes for Rand, teaching at National University and I still had some time on my hands, so I decided to explore the film and TV industry.

The first day I checked into an agency I was told to stand in a crowd scene, which I did. After that I was called to be in "Volcano," "Bulworth" and "Most Wanted" and more. I was also asked if I could be in several television shows and commercials. It's easy to do. You could do it too. If you want a major role, you have to have a single agent representing you. I was just doing this for fun. Most stars were smiley faced and made small talk to the people. The rules that had to be adhered to was not to take the star's pictures or ask for their autograph. My main responsibilities were Rand Institute contracting and teaching. The agencies even paid me for sitting in the audience of Judge Judy's court room and some daytime talk shows. A person stood out of the camera's view and held up signs saying: "laugh," "be angry," or "applaud."

On one of my trips from Los Angeles back to Silicon Valley, my attention was directed to a group of people approaching a nearby airport gate. I saw it was Ringo Starr and his wife and entourage. I approached Ringo and asked him for his autograph. I was glad I had a napkin and pen to put in front of him. He looked at me for what seemed like a long time, as he took a puff from a cigarette. He must have been in a good mood from that puff of cigarette because he wrote his name and the year on the napkin. He handed me the napkin and gave me the peace sign. His wife was the last Bond girl and she still looked beautiful. He was so nice.

Here are some tips on the west coast. The Getty art museum and the Hearst Castle are two places worth spending your time. The Getty is known for its art, architecture and gardens. The Hearst Castle has a considerable collection of art and antiques and wild animals in the yards. All visitors were protected by the bus. There are missions you should see all the way up the coast. Saint Junipero Serra established missions all along the coast and lived at Carmel mission until he died. He is in a sarcophagus you can see in the mission and several Indian graves are outside the mission from the 1500s. Carmel is where Doris Day and Clint Eastwood lived. Clint Eastwood opened a restaurant called The Hog's Breath, which annoyed some of the snobby locals. He was elected mayor for a while, and changed the law so that you can eat ice cream on the street. There are many nice hotels and places to eat in Carmel. Although Serra continued to establish missions up the coast, Stanford University, located in Palo Alto, Silicon Valley, has not only a mission to observe, but it also has but a Rodin garden for you to enjoy. Of course, you should see the Hoover Institute, which is also there.

Hearst Castle Pool

Carmel Mission

San Francisco is such a wonderful place that many books are about it alone. There are bright colors to look at on the buildings and houses and cable cars to ride by them all. It is worth standing in line to get Ghirardelli chocolate. Fisherman's Wharf offers sourdough bread bowls with clam chowder in it. There are boat rides also offered so you can see huge navy ships and Alcatraz. The crookedest steps in the world are there and a China and Japan town. There is an old glamorous hotel called the Mark Hopkins. Many refer to it as "the Mark." I stay there often. The top floor is a restaurant surrounded by glass so you can see the whole city. Car shows are often across the street at the Fairmont Hotel. The Fairmont has a famous tiki bar called the Tonga Room in the basement and a dance floor. Straight down the hill from the Mark is Union Square and famous shopping place and cable cars can keep you going everywhere. If you're a beer lover, go to a place called the Toronado in the Lower Haight. I think they have about fifty beers on their menu board every day. A reasonably priced place for good food where you can sit out on the water is called Reds Java and it's on the Embarcadero near the Bay Bridge.

Buena Vista San Francisco

Cable Car

Also look for Gilroy, which hosts the Garlic Festival. I never knew so many things could be made to taste like garlic: ice cream, corn on the cob and beer were all things you would find there, and they were tasty too.

If you continue up the coast you will run into the Napa Valley. Napa has a lot of fine wineries, which are pleasurable. A lot of the wineries offer cheese with samples of their various wines. They also have a winery that makes champagne.

Squaw Valley is a winter resort. I liked to go up there on weekends. If it's very warm out, they will have man made snow and some people ski in their bathing suits. The Olympics were held there long ago.

The last area I'll mention is Sacramento, the capital of California. Sacramento has a lot of cool buildings, cruises on the Sacramento River and a great train exhibit.

I want to tell you how close Reno and Las Vegas are to Silicon Valley. Most people fly to those places but you can drive if you don't mind a long drive. My tips would be to tell you to stick to the shows, the one-armed bandits and the buffets. The people who play the table games make the real money and I'm not pushing for that because the House usually wins. In Las Vegas there are lots of things to do. I went up in a small plane and saw the Grand Canyon, Hoover Dam and Colorado River. There are often tour buses that go to Reno which is known as the Biggest Little City in the World. It's a mini-Las Vegas.

Las Vegas Strip

Living in California is like being on vacation every day.

It's time to give you some information on eastern cities. I'll just pick a few hot-spots, because I spent most of my time in California.

You should go to Buffalo, New York. That's where Buffalo wings originated and it's very close to Niagara Falls, which is very scenic.

Niagara Falls

Next, I would suggest going to Manhattan, New York City. One time we arrived at the hotel and we were late, not our fault. The clerk had given our room away and we could not look for another room that late at night. I did not hear money exchange hands, but I did hear the desk clerk say, "well I guess you can stay in Michael Jackson's suite, but don't be handsy about everything." And she laughed. I thought she was only kidding, but we went to the room and it was like the inside of a house. There was a beautiful dining room, a living room, den, bedroom, and bathroom. The windows looked out on the beautiful city. I still thought the desk clerk had been kidding until I saw the beautiful baby grand piano in the den, so now I don't know. Pizza is great in New York as long as you don't buy it from a chain. A really good place for deli food is Katz' Deli in the textile district, and is the place where When Harry Met Sally was filmed. New York has many good Broadway shows and the off-Broadway is also good. The last time I went to an off-Broadway show is when Woody Harrelson was there and he talked to us all at intermission.

Pittsburgh, Pennsylvania is a gorgeous town. It has two funiculars called inclines that go up to Mt. Washington where you can look down on the city, the three rivers that connect at Point State Park and all the bridges. A popular place to visit is the Strip District, which is loaded with dozens of ethnic stores and yes, Pittsburgh is the original place where Primanti's put fries and coleslaw in its sandwiches. A lot of other places have tried to mimic it, but the original is here. Pitt, Duquesne and Carnegie Mellon University (CMU) are located there. CMU also has satellite campuses across the world. The students are super smart and robotics is studied there. California University is also in Pennsylvania and graduates a lot of teachers.

Washington, DC should always be visited when you get a chance. There's so much there to see and do. The Capitol, the Smithsonian, plus all the memorials are worth seeing and a lot of them are free.

Capitol

Philadelphia has a lot of history, like the Liberty Bell and Independence Hall. While you're there you have to have a Philly cheesesteak.

God bless those who are still trying to recover from hurricane Michael. The east coast has to worry about tornados, hurricanes, and more while the west coast has to worry about earthquakes, tsunamis, flooding and more. All the world has concerns with weather.

South Beach, Miami Florida is very hip. There are lots of places to eat and club, and you are bound to run into celebrities. A lot of the restaurants have outside dining because across the street is the ocean. The Art Deco hotels are gorgeous to look at.

South Beach Miami

The Florida Keys are below Miami and you can drive to them or go straight to them by plane. The farthest away is Key West. It's the southernmost point in the continental United States. You should go to Hemmingway's House and see the descendants of his many six-toed cats. You can also see Sloppy Joes bar for a lot of entertainment. There's also the Truman Annex, which is where Harry Truman stayed when he wanted to get away. What's really unusual is that a lot of the dining is done outside and chickens approach food and it is frowned upon to chase them away.

Hemmingway House

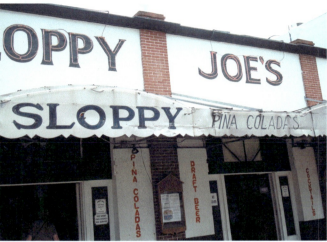

Sloppy Joes Key West

Truman Little White House

I think lastly, I'll write about a southern city called New Orleans. What's nice is you can go most anywhere and there's live music. We boated down a swamp and they gave us a tiny alligator to pet on the way. You have to try the food especially the po-boy and the muffuletta sandwiches, and the beignets, which are a great desert.

New Orleans Alligator

I will give you some information on Hawaii. I know Hawaii has a lot of islands and each island is noted for something. The last island formed there happened when a volcano spilled over and there is black sand everywhere. There's and island for the whole family to enjoy and that's the big island. It rains a lot in Kuai so it's known as the green island. Maui seems to be the island where most honeymooners go. I was in a rental car in Maui, when I saw Robin Williams riding a bike. I pulled over and he very nicely, but briefly, chatted with me. Then I got back in my car and I saw the nanny with Robin's child's stroller and they waved when I waved goodbye. May Robin rest in currently. A lot of people from Silicon Valley got to Hawaii for Christmas. Mele Kalikimaka is the thing to say on bright Hawaiian Christmas day. That's Merry Christmas to you. Hawaii has a lot of hula dancing when you go out to dinner and always order the Kobe beef.

You don't have to fly or walk to go someplace, you can go on a cruise ship like we did two times. The first cruise was of the eastern Caribbean and included the Bahamas, Puerto Rico, Grand Turk and St. Thomas. The Bahamas reminds me of Hawaii because of the clear, warm water. It's also easy to rent mopeds there and they are fun to ride. In San Juan, Puerto Rico, we took a bus tour to see the sights. It was interesting to find out about how they would like to vote in U.S. elections, but they don't because they would have to pay U.S. taxes. Grand Turk had beautiful beaches and St. Thomas had beautiful views. Both of my cruises embarked in Miami. The second cruise was of the western Caribbean and included Cozumel, Belize, Honduras and Grand Cayman. When we were taken to Grand Cayman, we were put on a boat and went snorkeling. We toured all of them like we did the first cruise and remember to take on your cruise both casual and dress clothes, depending on where you go for dinner. You'll get a menu and entertainment when you go to the dressy restaurants and good food when you go to the casual ones too. No reservations are necessary at the casual ones. I have gone to more cities and countries but I would never get this book published, so I'll stop at cruises. I hope I've incited you to go to some of these places, but remember, no matter where you go, there's no place like home. LOL.

Carnival Glory Cruiseship

St. Thomas

Grand Turk from cruise